THE

HEALING, DELIVERANCE, AND TRANSFORMATIVE

POWER OF

PSALM

30

Prayers to turn impossible situations around

Jeffrey Okaekwu

Prayer Requests and Counseling

Send me an email at prayercdmcfamily@gmail.com if you need prayer. We have praying team that will intercede for you at all times.

Or

Visit our prayer group on Facebook

CDMC DAILY PRAYERS AND DEVOTIONALS.. a home of joy

We would love to stand with you in

prayers

Reference

New King James Version

Table of Contents

INTRODUCTION

Psalm 30 is written to draw the healing, deliverance, and transforming power of God into situations for radical change.

It starts with thanksgiving and ends with thanksgiving to God for his marvelous work of healing, deliverance, restoration, transformation, and salvation from physical death.

This psalm has been proven to move the hand of God urgently into situations and this book unfolds the mysteries behind every verse of this psalm to guide you with an effective prayer of deliverance, healing, and divine transformation.

It contains other scriptures connected to the verses to explain deep mysteries from them and prayer points after every verse to move the power of God into action.

It is a great psalm to pray off strange and troubling occurrences in your life.

Pray these prayers with fasting to build a strong spiritual root in them.

The pressure will force open and clear off unwanted things in your life that will bring glory to God.

Pray it to change that situation now in Jesus' name

Chapter one

Build your confidence in the strength of God

Verse 1

"1 I will extol thee, O LORD; for thou hast lifted me up, and hast not made my foes to rejoice over me."

The psalmist built his confidence in the strength of God for he knows that God's strength will never allow any situations to swallow him or evil attacks to bring him down.

He praises God with all his heart because his deliverance power is working in his life causing him to overcome his enemies at all times.

This explains better what the scripture says about God in psalm 127:1

"Unless the LORD builds a house, the work of the builders is wasted. Unless the LORD protects a city, guarding it with sentries will do no good."

The same power of God that protects you from evil agendas is the same power that will lift you up beyond your imagination when you put your confidence in him.

Daniel was not moved when an evil agenda was placed against him by some evil men instead he put his confidence in the strength of God who later gave him victory over their evil plots and promoted him after the victory... (Daniel 6)

This is what God can do for the one that puts his/her confidence and trust in him.

Pray these prayers of faith and move good evening power of God unto action

a) I receive divine strength now in Jesus' name

b) God, my confidence is built on you for my transformation in Jesus' name

c) I trust you to take care of my situation now by mercy in Jesus' name

d) Lift me up beyond my imagination in Jesus' name

e) Do something new in my life now in Jesus' name

f) Fill me with inner strength to move higher now in Jesus' name

g) Do not allow the plans of the wicked ones to prevail over my life in Jesus' name

Chapter Two

Place an order for the healing power of God

Verse 2

"O LORD my God, I cried unto thee, and thou hast healed me."

This verse describes God's nature in two ways

a) **THE NATURE TO HEAR SOMEONE'S CRY FOR HELP AND RESPOND IMMEDIATELY**

God does not like to see someone in pain or trouble so He finds a way to reach out to them and give them a helping hand .he does this to make them see that they can trust him to help out and restore back peace and joy in their lives.

This was clearly written in Psalm 91:14-16

"14 Because he hath set his love upon me, therefore will I deliver him: I will set him on high because he hath known my name.

15 He shall call upon me, and I will answer him: I will be with him in trouble; I will deliver him, and honor him.

16 With long life will I satisfy him and shew him my salvation?"

He wants you to play a part in this by knowing his name which means understanding that he is able to do all things and that includes taking away your pains and burdens.

So when you know this and stir up your faith in him, then he will come in and take away that pain or trouble in your life and honor you after doing that.

This was what blind Bartimaeus did when he heard that Jesus was passing by...Mark 10:46

He cried out to him with a loud voice and did not stop crying even when he was told by the disciples of Jesus Christ to stop making noise.

He drew the attention of Jesus Christ to his situation by crying out for help for God is moved when one cries out for help to him from the bottom of his/ her heart.

That was exactly what blind Bartimaeus did on that day and won himself a miracle from Christ Jesus.

B) THE SECOND NATURE OF GOD THAT (VERSE 2) OF PSALM 30 REVEALS IS THAT GOD IS A GREAT HEALER AND HE CAN HEAL ALL KINDS OF SICKNESSES.

The psalmist cried out with joy that God has healed him from his sickness just like the man at the beautiful gate shouted out when he was completely healed by God through the power in the name of Jesus Christ...Acts 3:2

This is an indication that yours is not exceptional and can be healed completely when you put your trust and faith in him.

The sickness can be so terrible like the doctor's report said but God's report says "NO" to that just like the scripture says in Luke 18:27

Jesus replied, "What is impossible with man is possible with God."

So cry out with these prayer points and move the healing power of God into that sickness now

a) Heal me from my sickness oh God in Jesus' name

b) Heal my broken heart and comfort me with joy now in Jesus' name

c) Heal my wounds now and cause me to trust you more in Jesus' name

d) Save me from evil attacks in Jesus' name

e) Deliver me from falling in Jesus' name

f) Take away pains and fears from me and grant me peace on every side in life in Jesus' name

g) Restore good health in my life now in Jesus' name

Chapter three

Cancel untimely deaths in your life and family

Verse 3

"O LORD, thou hast brought up my soul from the grave: thou hast kept me alive, that I should not go down to the pit."

This is a great declaration from the psalmist that God is his deliverer and his savior who never let him stay down to death whenever he falls sick like Psalms 118: 13-14

"13 Thou hast thrust sore at me that I might fall: but the LORD helped me.

14 The LORD is my strength and song, and is become my salvation."

His plan is to see that we fulfill our destiny without interruption from the wicked ones stated in John 10:10

"10 The thief cometh not, but for to steal, and to kill, and to destroy: I am come that they might have life and that they might have it more abundantly."

The picture of this is seen in the story of the adulterous woman who was about to be stoned to death by some group of men who felt she has broken the law of the land and deserved death but Jesus intervened and told the woman that he has not come to destroy but to save...John 8:1

The authority has already been given to you by God to keep declaring abundantly life into dead-looking situations in your life by the power in Jesus' name like Psalm 118: 17

"17 I shall not die, but live, and declare the works of the LORD"

Pray with prayer points and declare that this will be your option and that of your loved ones in Jesus' name

a) I reject untimely death in Jesus' name

b) I claim abundant life for me and my loved ones now in Jesus' name

c) I claim divine preservation of God now in Jesus' name

d) I cover my life with the blood of Jesus

d) I cover my going outs and coming ins daily with the special blood of Jesus Christ

e) No evil shall befall me in Jesus name

f) I will live to keep revealing God's glory in my life in Jesus' name

g) Lord, make my life a living testimony before people in Jesus' name

Chapter Four

Declare his transformation power in your situation

Verse 4 & 5

"4 Sing unto the LORD, O ye saints of his, and give thanks at the remembrance of his holiness.

5 For his anger endureth but a moment; in his favor is life: weeping may endure for a night, but joy cometh in the morning."

God's anger rose upon the people of Nineveh when he could no longer tolerate their sinful acts and he sent his prophet JONAH to warn them of their sinful acts and what He would do to them if they fail to desist from them.

When they heard it, they repented from their sinful ways to the ways that pleased God and JONAH became furious at the fact that God shows great mercy and compassion to the ones that ask for his mercy from their heart and repent from their sinful ways...Jonah 4:1

2 Chronicles 7:14

"if my people, who are called by my name, will humble themselves and pray and seek my face and turn from their wicked ways, then I will hear from heaven, and I will forgive their sin and will heal their land."

This is what brings about great FAVORS of God in someone's life. At this moment, he forgives and heals the person from spiritual and physical wounds caused by sin, and by doing that, he takes away weeping, fears and depression from the life of such person and replaces them with joy and abundant life.

Finally, he puts a new song in that person's mouth to sing out for joy to the glory of his name

Pray with these prayer points and bless his holy name for his mercy endures forever.

a) I receive divine transformation now in Jesus' name

b) I am more than a conqueror in Jesus' name

c) My situation will never bring me down rather my God will be revealed through it in Jesus' name

d) I'm stronger and greater than that situation in Jesus' mighty name

e) I am divinely favored in Jesus' name

f) This is my time to shine in Jesus' name

g) This is my moment of unspeakable joy and nothing will ever take that away from you in Jesus' name

h) I will live always to glorify the name of my Lord in my situations in Jesus' name

I) The Lord has given me victory over that situation in Jesus' name

Chapter five

Stand and stay strong in him

Verse 6

"6 And in my prosperity I said, I shall never be moved."

In this verse, the psalmist is standing strong in God and not allowing the blessings of God in his life to move him away from him.

It is a declaration from the psalmist telling God that he will not be distracted from following him when his blessings start increasing in his life.

He also knows that it is in the power of God to lift one up and in his power to bring one down...psalm 75:7

This is clearly written in **Deuteronomy 30:9**

"Then the Lord your God will prosper you abundantly in all the work of your hand, in the offspring of your body and in the offspring of your cattle and in the produce of your ground, for the Lord will again rejoice over you for good, just as He rejoiced over your fathers"

The psalmist declares in this verse that his financial blessings will never take him away from loving and serving God.

With this, he is telling God that he is everything to him and nothing would change that.

Pray these prayers to stand firm in God

a) Grant me the inner strength to stay strong in you oh God in Jesus' name

b) Fill my spirit with fire that will burn always for you in Jesus' name

c) Build my trust in him with signs and wonders in Jesus' name

d) Cause me not to deviate from you in Jesus' name

e) Grant me strength to keep overcoming the world and temptation that it throws at me in Jesus' name

f) Help me to stay focused on you in Jesus' name

g) Grant me grace and wisdom to understand your ways and follow them in Jesus' name

h) Do not let me be distracted by your blessings in Jesus' name

Chapter six
Call for divine favor in your situation

Verse 7

"LORD, by thy favor thou hast made my mountain to stand strong:"

The mountain there represents great height and growth in one's endeavor.

The psalmist found favor in the sight of God when he experienced a great lifting up.

He was lifted from a wilderness state to a glorious state.

He declares that God's favor has kept him growing from one level to another level without falling as he did in the life of Isaac in Genesis 26:12

"Isaac planted crops in that land and the same year reaped a hundredfold because the LORD blessed him."

Pray these prayers for the favor of God and grace to keep growing in your endeavors

a) I stand on a solid rock in you in Jesus' name

b) I will never fall or be shaken by my situations because I have you in my life in Jesus' name

c) I will never be moved by the activities of dark forces against my life in Jesus' name

d) I will never be pulled down in Jesus' name

e) The lord is my strength and my salvation; nothing can take that away from me in Jesus' name

f) The lord is with me, who can be against me in Jesus' name

g) I've found great favor in the sight of my God in Jesus' name

h) The lord is my shepherd, I shall never want in Jesus' name

Chapter Seven
Defeat your fears

Verse 7b

"thou didst hide thy face, and I was troubled."...(Verse 7b)

This is a declaration to ask the lord to appear in your situation and deliver you from all that troubles you.

The psalmist wrote that because he needed the urgent attention of God to come out of a situation that has been troubling him Psalm 70:1 says

"Make haste, O God, to deliver me! O LORD, make haste to help me!"

This is also a prayer telling God to appear in your situation so that people will believe that he is the lord of your life like he did in the life of Daniel when he was thrown into the lion's den. Daniel 6 and the lives of Shadrach, Meshach, and Abednego when they were thrown into the fiery furnace...Daniel 3:16

Pray these prayer points to receive urgent intervention from God in your situation

a) I defeat the spirit of fear in my life now in Jesus' name

b) I command every arrow of fear shot into my life to come out now in Jesus' name

c) I receive boldness in my spirit now in Jesus' name

d) Appear in my situation oh God, by your mercy now in Jesus' name

e) Defend your name in my life God in Jesus' name

f) Show yourself mighty and powerful in my situation now in the mighty name of Jesus name

g) I uproot whatever is not planted by God in my life now in Jesus name

Chapter Eight

Return God's words in your life back to him

Verse 8 & 9

"8 I cried to thee, O LORD; and unto the LORD I made supplication.

9 What profit is there in my blood when I go down to the pit? Shall the dust praise thee? Shall it declare thy truth?"

This is a prayer request for God's protection and preservation in your life.

The psalmist is asking for long life and deliverance from untimely death like his word says in **_psalm 118:17-18_**

"17 I shall not die, but live, and declare the works of the LORD.

18 The LORD hath chastened me sore: but he hath not given me over unto death."

This is a prayer telling God that he should not let untimely death come your way or come to your loved ones rather he should reveal his glory through your life always so that people will see and glorify God in your life.

This is what he said in *1 Corinthians 2:9*

"9 But as it is written, Eye hath not seen, nor ear heard, neither have entered into the heart of man, the things which God hath prepared for them that love him."

So stand in the authority of these words and tell God that you love him and these words that he spoke here are for you and your loved ones to the glory of his name in your life and in your home.

Pray these prayers and ask him for life in abundance with good health

a) May your promises come to pass in my life now in Jesus' name

b) May your words be made manifest in my situation now in Jesus' name

c) I will not die but live to reveal your glory in my life in Jesus' name

d) I receive good health and great transformation in my life in Jesus' name

e) Restore back all that the enemy take from me by your mercy in Jesus' name

f) Restore peace back in my life and remove whatever troubles me from my life in Jesus' name

Chapter Nine

Ask for his mercy in your situation

Verse 10

"10 Hear, O LORD, and have mercy upon me: LORD, be thou, my helper."

Hannah prayed this prayer when she couldn't conceive and the pressure coming from her co-wife against her condition was too much for her to bear....1 Samuel 1:9

The Lord appeared in her situation as her helper and glorified his name by making her the mother of children.

Some of us are in a condition that demands God coming to help us out before it gets out of hand.

If you are in such condition, then give him back his word in Psalm 40:11

"Do not withhold your mercy from me, Lord; may your love and faithfulness always protect me."

And ask him to attend to your situation that you need his urgent intervention as your helper.

Pray these prayers

a) Look upon my situation oh God with your eyes of mercy

b) Have mercy upon me and my loved ones and show us kindness now in Jesus' name

c) I receive divine help now in Jesus' mighty name

d) Today, I receive the powerful touch of God in my life and situation now in Jesus' name

e) May your mercy follow me all the days of my life in Jesus' name

f) Attend to my situation urgently by your mercy in Jesus' name

Chapter Ten

Call for divine transformation

Verse 11

"Thou hast turned for me my mourning into dancing: thou hast put off my sackcloth, and girded me with gladness;"

This is seen in the story of Joseph who was put into prison for a crime he did not commit and he was made to stay there permanently by Potiphar, a man of authority in Egypt whose wife framed Joseph that he attempted to rape her...Genesis 39:19

What happened to Joseph from the life he lived in his father's house to the life he lived in the Egyptian prison was a process of going from good to bad which this verse describes as putting on sackcloth; but God is faithful to bring to pass his word and promises In your life by pulling off your sackcloth and replacing it with the garment of glory like **Romans 8:28-30** says

"28 And we know that all things work together for good to them that love God, to them who are the called according to his purpose.

29 For whom he did foreknow, he also did predestinate to be conformed to the image of his Son, that he might be the firstborn among many brethren.

30 Moreover whom he did predestinate, them he also called: and whom he called, them he also justified: and whom he justified, them he also glorified.

Joseph fell into this category and when it was time for God to fulfill his word in his life and glorify his name, he troubled the king's palace by giving Pharaoh a disturbing dream that finally caused the destiny of Joseph to be fulfilled and not to be destroyed by the enemy...Genesis 41:1

What God did with Pharaoh and Joseph was to bring forth a connection that looks so impossible which is connecting a king also seen as a president in his country and a prisoner to work together.

God caused King Pharaoh to break protocol for the sake of Joseph when he commanded that Joseph be released and brought to him immediately.

God used Pharaoh to remove the sackcloth that was worn on Joseph in the prison and put on him the garment of honor.

God did all that to prove that our destiny is not in the hands of the enemy but in his hands, and the moment we trust him in all we do, he will guide us to fulfill it.

This verse declares what God did in the life of Joseph as turning someone's mourning into dancing and the same God is able to do the same in your life if you believe.

Pray these prayers; asking God for great transformation in your life

a) I receive divine transformation now in Jesus' name

b) I'm free from every bondage and manipulation of the enemy in Jesus' name

c) My sorrows are turned to joy now in Jesus' name

d) The lord has worn me a garment of honor in Jesus' name

e) The lord has lifted me up by the power in the name of Jesus Christ

f) The lord has granted my requests in Jesus' name

g) The lord has brought great joy into my life now in Jesus' name

h) He has put a new song in my mouth in Jesus' name

Chapter Eleven

Ask for his glory to be revealed in your situation

Verse 12

"To the end that my glory may sing praise to thee, and not be silent. O LORD my God, I will give thanks unto thee forever."

One thing that God will never stop doing is glorifying his name in people's life.

He is not a God that will sit and not do anything about people's situations and problems.

He created this earth mainly to always reveal his glory in people's lives.

This can be seen in these two chapters of the Bible

2 Corinthians 3:18

"And we all, with unveiled faces, beholding the glory of the Lord, are being transformed into the same image from one degree of glory to another, for this comes from the Lord who is the Spirit.'

1 Chronicles 16:24

Declare his glory among the nations, his marvelous works among all the peoples!

The psalmist returned the word of God and his promises in his life back to him by telling him he is a

God of glory who is always glorifying his name in the lives of his people so he asked Him to glorify his name in his situation that his glory in his life is seen by people and not be silenced.

He is equally telling God to cause his name to be glorified in his life.

When you pray with this verse, you tell God to cause his healing and deliverance power to come upon your situation so that people will see it and glorify his name in your life.

This request goes with songs of praise and thanksgiving to God like the psalmist did in that verse.

Pray with these prayer points

a) May your glory radiate in my life always in Jesus' name

b) May your fire burn higher in my spirit in Jesus' name

c) Open my eyes go keep seeing reasons to glorify your name in Jesus' name

d) May people see your beauty in my life and situations in Jesus' name

e) May your peace never depart from me in Jesus' name

f) Cause me to always cry out for joy in all I do in Jesus' name

g) My glory will never be covered in Jesus' name

h) I will keep seeing reasons to give you thanks in Jesus' name

I) put testimonies in my mouth in Jesus' name

J) Bless my life always and cause me to dance in Jesus' mighty name

K) Thank you for granting my requests in Jesus' name

AMEN

Conclusion

I pray that you receive great transformation now in Jesus' name.

God is too faithful to fail you, I pray that he fulfills his promises in your life, marriage, work, and in your family to his glory in Jesus' name.

I decree into your life, abundant grace, blessings, glory, and complete wholeness in your health in Jesus' name.

I prophesy that you receive miracles and testimonies now and forever in Jesus' name.

May the Lord open great doors for you and lead you into success now by his grace in Jesus' name, AMEN

You can share your testimony with us or request deliverance prayer with CDMC family prayer warriors by sending an email to: prayercdmcfamily@gmail.com

Or

Partner with the CDMC family evangelical movement to deliver souls and win them back to God by sending emails to: partnercdmcfamily@gmail.com

You can subscribe to our YouTube channel to receive words of faith, details of my deliverance books, healing and deliverance programs, and testimonies of people touched by the power of God.

https://m.youtube.com/channel/UComoe_ERocg_7gZ

KiUWfSfA

Thank you and God bless you